A JOURNALIST LOOKS AT THE LORD'S PRAYER

English

Our Father

who art in heaven,
hallowed be thy name.
Thy kingdom come
Thy will be done,
on earth as it is in heaven.
Give us this day our daily bread;
and forgive us our trespasses,
as we forgive those who trespass
    against us,
and lead us not into temptation,
but deliver us from evil.
Amen.

JAMES ANTONELLIS

A JOURNALIST LOOKS AT THE LORD'S PRAYER

The Our Father in the mass media

St Paul Publications

Original title: *Nonostante tutto "Osiamo dire"*
Copyright © 1990 Edizioni Paoline s.r.l., Cinisello
Balsamo, Italy.

Translated by Thomas Kala

Cover design by Diane Edward

St Paul Publications
Middlegreen, Slough SL3 6BT, United Kingdom

English translation © St Paul Publications UK 1991

ISBN 085439 384 6

Printed by The Guernsey Press Co Ltd, Guernsey. C.I.

St Paul Publications is an activity of the priests and
brothers of the Society of St Paul who proclaim the Gospel
through the media of social communication

Contents

THE LORD'S PRAYER
IN VARIOUS LANGUAGES

Foreword

This book argues persuasively that the Our Father has a universal application: its horizons, says James Antonellis, are 'vast enough to encompass all nations and religions'.

Maybe so; but as a journalist working mainly in the field of religion, I take the heretical view that what divides believers is often more interesting than what unites them.

As a small child, I remember someone sending my devoutly Catholic grandmother a Christmas card which, for some eccentric reason, incorporated the words of the Lord's Prayer. 'Our Father', it began, 'which art in heaven'. My grandmother was puzzled. 'You would have thought they would have known better', she said disapprovingly.

It is a small point, but it still amuses me. Until a few years ago, Catholics said 'who there was another difference: non-catholics always appended the line about 'thine is the kingdom', which, however edifying, is not part of the text, as it were.

But times have changed. These days, English-speaking Protestants tend to use the Catholic version, beginning with 'who art' and ending with 'deliver us from evil'. Not an earth-shattering change, perhaps, but I can think of few more effective illustrations of the coming together of Christian traditions. Unlike many other ecumenical developments, it is the sort of thing people notice.

For most of its history, of course, Catholics have said the Lord's Prayer in Latin. Indeed, it happens to be the only prayer I know by heart in that language – which is not very impressive, but one more Latin prayer than most of my contemporaries know, in my experience.

At university I occasionally made rather shameful use of this fact. As a Catholic, I was sometimes called upon to say 'a Latin grace' at the more self-conscious sort of undergraduate dinner party. Rather than confess ignorance, I would rattle out the Lord's Prayer at machine-gun speed, and very well it worked, too – until someone correctly identified it. But I was not alone, I discovered only the other day, much to my surprise, I heard someone else stand up at dinner and launch into the *Pater Noster*. I didn't have the heart to say anything.

A final thought: one might imagine that what this book calls 'the most sublime of prayers' would inspire composers, as all the other great prayers of the Christian Church have. Far from it. The only musical settings of the Lord's Prayer I have come across have been barbarous congregational settings which serve only to diminish its effect. One version in particular sounds disconcertingly like 'It's a long way to Tipperary.'

But never mind: the simple fact is that the words themselves possess an eloquence which renders any other medium unnecessary. That, at any rate, is the conclusion I came to after reading this remarkable book.

DAMIAN THOMPSON
Religious Affairs Correspondent
The Daily Telegraph

Latin

Pater noster

qui es in cælis:

sanctificetur nomen tuum;

adveniat regnum tuum;

fiat voluntas tua, sicut in cælo et
in terra.

Panem nostrum cotidianum da
nobis hodie;

et dimitte nobis debita nostra,

sicut et nos dimittimus
debitoribus nostris,

et ne nos inducas in tentationem,

sed libera nos a malo.

Amen.

Introduction

Is journalism a difficult profession? Perhaps. Or is it better described as fascinating, often adventurous, always serious? It is certainly a profession which presupposes a sense of responsibility. For, although people may become journalists for all kinds of reasons, what they really want is to communicate to the world and shape public opinion.

Is it then a vocation, an apostolate, a mission? It is rather an undertaking in which the urge to affirm one's personality finds expression in informing and influencing the public. This, in any case, is reflected in the ideal of both secular and Christian journalists. And this social responsibility is recognised by all. Moreover, some 150 years ago Hegel declared that 'the reading of the newspaper has become modern man's morning prayer.' Hegel's statement might give a different perspective to what happens around us daily; it might also lead us to modify our attitude at the office, at the scene of an event and the filing of every report. This change of attitude is, for those who believe, an important step towards loving God and neighbour. It is almost a prayer.

In this context, it is worth recalling what Georges Bernanos wrote in his *Diary of a Country Priest:* 'The desire to pray is in itself a prayer.' Such an affirmation comes as a revelation to me, a truant from the school of prayer, a professional journalist and writer concerned with the daily news and the course of history, an individual caught up with the frenzy of a superficial society, a man consumed by personal and communal passions or distracted at times by interests and ambitions and at other times lost in dreams and private thoughts. The desire to pray is in itself a prayer. I find this most encouraging, and it is something I want to emphasise, for I don't know how to pray.

When I say that I don't know how to pray, I do not in any way feel guilty. To each one the good Lord has assigned talents and handicaps according to the mysterious balance that sustains the universe. In the timetable of my everyday life the space I have allotted to prayer is pretty minuscule. It does not mean that I can do without prayer. Within me there is a continuing tension between the flesh that ties me down and the spirit that wants to rise above earthly things. Of course, given the right circumstances, I would not hesitate to say the rosary, recite the litanies learned in childhood or repeat mechanically the formulae that accompany every religious rite. But how genuine are such prayers? Can they really put us in touch with our Creator? I doubt it.

I have always imagined that prayer leads us out of our world without mixing our plans and problems with the designs of God. I feel that a prayer of petition for ourselves, our family or friends could almost be blasphemous. It is like a deal. 'Lord, I believe in you, but I would appreciate acknowledgement of my faith in you.' The very thought of such a 'contract' I find disturbing. However, I realise that I am incapable of total detachment from the world and self-abandonment to God who is the source of all life.

I admit that I do not know how to pray, but at the same time I admire (and perhaps also envy) those to whom prayer comes naturally. I think of the saints utterly absorbed in their encounter with the Lord. Their meetings take place, without even the hint of a distraction, in the reading of a text, through mnemonic aids, in silence, in colloquy, or in the simple prostration of the body.

I do not know how to pray. I am distracted. I read without due attention, pursuing parallel thoughts and searching for a logic behind formulae. I lack the mystical sustaining power and I fail to grasp the link between gestures and words. I am tormented by the abysmal distance between the crude language of my faith and the edifying piety of the writers of the Early Church or of those mediaeval religious communities or of the vibrant postconciliar groups of today.

I don't know how to pray. I am lacking in perseverance. I have no discipline. Of course, true prayer does not consist in words, as St Augustine has taught: true prayer comes from the heart. And Jesus himself has warned us: 'When you are praying, do not heap up empty phrases as the Gentiles do; for they think that they will be heard because of their many words' (Matthew 6:7). For this reason I like to take refuge in silence from time to time as, for example, when I walk by myself to the office, making my peace with nature and exorcising the demons of noise. Then, and in similar circumstances, I return to the only prayer which I know well and which I love deeply: the Our Father or the Lord's Prayer.

We usually recite – or rather, as the liturgy puts it – we have the courage to say – the text from Jesus' Sermon on the Mount (Matthew 6:9-13). There is another version in the Gospel of Luke (11:2-4), which modifies some of the phrases in the prayer and places it within Jesus' teaching on the Mount of Olives where today there is a church whose walls are covered with that same prayer in forty-five languages. In the first centuries of Christianity, however, a great deal of controversy surrounded the Lord's Prayer, due to the differing interpretations of thinkers like Tertullian in his *On Prayer,* Cyprian in his treatise *On the Lord's Prayer* and Augustine in his *Homilies.* But all exegetes agree that the Lord's Prayer is the most sublime of all prayers.

Maranatha, derived from the Syro-Aramaic liturgy, was popular among the early Christians. The word, which means 'Come, Lord Jesus', is the hallmark of St John in the Book of Revelation. It is a waiting for the quickening presence, the *Parousia,* which reveals the Creator in the soul of every believer and undermines the reasoning of the agnostic and the unbeliever. This cry of hope, which assumes a specific Messianic sense in St Paul (2 Corinthians 3:17), has also an eschatological dimension for the people of the year 2000. But above all it is an invitation to prayer. And how can we respond to it? Perhaps we could begin by reflecting on the sacredness of life, on the questions of existence, on how to do God's will, on the hope that sustains every single human activity. We can thus begin to pray with an act of will.

But what does it cost me to pray? Sitting by his bed of suffering, I put this blunt question to Carlo Carretto in the descending darkness of an autumn evening. His hermitage in the woods of Spello, in the heart of green Umbria, seemed shut off from the rest of the world at that hour. The little follower of Jesus smiled and, taking my hand, he fixed me with his piercing eyes. He thought for a moment and then began to speak softly. Prayer, he said, is an explosion of love between two beings. Prayer has its springs not on earth but in heaven. Prayer is song, praise, music, poetry, tears, agony, joy, contemplation – whatever exalts humanity. I have searched and found, he said more than once with that Franciscan simplicity that had characterised his entire life. From his hermitage he succeeded, for a quarter of a century, in sharing his insights and blessings with all those who came to him. His open hermitage, a challenge to the city, was a symbol of permanence on the wooded slopes of Umbria where you are beckoned to prayer by every thicket, stream, rock and blue streak of sky. In this undulating country, as in the desolation of the Sahara and the tempting corridors of power in Rome, he held on to the motto of his life: Seek that you may find. Following in the footsteps of the saint of Assisi, he found God everywhere.

The story of Carlo Carretto's vocation helps us to understand better the value of prayer. Let us pick out the principal stages of his life: his upbringing in a humble and profoundly religious family; his involvement in Catholic Action in Italy; and the call of the desert to seek God through contemplation and poverty. These stages are essential for his 'journey without frontiers' in search of God. The ideal that inspired him was certainly unusual. He definitely did not want a Catholic domination of society; instead he worked incessantly for the transformation of hearts so that they would be open to universal love.

One of his lasting preoccupations was to see the priestly ministry exercised by all the faithful. He disliked all institutional taboos surrounding the priesthood. 'The Lord has given me,' he said, 'the charism of celibacy, and I am moved to tears of joy every time I thank him for this gift. I am happy in the solitude of my cell, but I cannot tolerate the insinuation in the Church that my status is special or more perfect than the others. True perfection consists in love, in prayer, in union with God – not in celibacy.' Priests are therefore valued not because of their status but because of their practice of faith, hope and charity. It then follows that the seminaries of today are to be found, above all, in religious movements whose members witness to the faith while facing the same problems as others in the world. At this stage

God is before our very eyes and we cannot miss him. Carlo Carretto liked to quote an old Jewish saying: 'A fish never sees the water in which it lives.' At every step we meet the Lord, but we brush past without sensing his presence.

Carretto approached every question with simplicity, sincerity and gentleness. I was impressed by the absence of prudishness in his speech. He spoke freely about his youthful days, his brief crushes and loves, his recognition of a woman's importance in a man's life. His heart had never been arid because he saw in the Song of Songs the symbol of woman as the indissoluble part of a man's life. Moreover, Carretto's spirituality was centred round everyday problems.

It was his wont to suggest for meditation his experiences in the desert with its carpet of sand and canopy of stars. Once, for example, in some remote part of Africa a feast was in full swing after the baptism of a convert, and the fire of the Holy Spirit seemed to have descended on the group. But everyone was conscious of the fact that there was no one to break bread in memory of Christ. From this episode he would lead to the logic of allowing the laity to conduct eucharistic services.

I shall remember Carlo Carretto as an authentic Christian who treated others as truly his brothers and sisters. Remembering him – as in the case of all other good and humble persons – I can calmly confess that I do not know how to pray. But I must also confess that I experience great joy whenever I manage to whisper: *Our Father...*

What is prayer? We find an admirable illustration of it in Job, that biblical personality who merits close study. He in fact teaches us the meaning of life itself. Accept good and evil with equanimity. Do not get worked up about the adversity of the just and the prosperity of the wicked. Trust God whose actions now will make sense only later. The poem of Job in the Bible is not a precise answer to the problem of human suffering. But it is certainly an invitation to hope rather than despair. 'Naked I came from my mother's womb, and naked shall I return; the Lord gave and the Lord has taken away; blessed be the name of the Lord'

(Job 1:21). And after his long dialogue with God, Job submits in an act of faith, adoration and love: 'I know that thou canst do all things, and that no purpose of thine can be thwarted' (Job 42:2).

Then there came Christ. His teaching on hope has undermined the old tradition of resignation and given a new creative impulse to life. Christian hope integrates humanity in the totality of matter and spirit, freeing everyone and guiding them along the path to fulfilment in society. The Second Vatican Council has rounded off the teaching on this topic thus: 'The laity has the noble task of striving to realise God's plan of salvation among all peoples everywhere on earth. Let lay people therefore adopt all the means necessary for an active participation in the Church's work of salvation' (*Lumen Gentium* 33). These are useful points to bear in mind.

But the question persists. What do we do when we pray? When we pray we entrust ourselves to God, establishing dialogue and seeking reassurance. In the lives of Jesus and the apostles prayer appears as a basic factor in the link between the human and the divine. Their prayer is always addressed to the Father, not to human intercessors. Following this tradition the Early Church took its inspiration from the apostles, the eucharistic celebrations, the Last Supper and indeed from the Lord's Prayer itself. The apostles have especially urged us to have recourse to the Father. Thus we read in St Paul's Letter to the Galatians: 'And because you are sons, God has sent the Spirit of his Son into our hearts, crying, "Abba! Father!"' (4:6). And in the Apostle's Letter to the Philippians: 'Have no anxiety about anything, but in everything let your requests be made known to God. And the peace of God, which passes all understanding, will keep your hearts and your minds in Christ Jesus' (4:6-7).

Prayer is thus a direct contact between us and God. It is a true dialogue. A dialogue of words and silences. Sometimes we ask and God may grant our wish; and at other times we ask and God may remain silent. God's ways are after all inscrutable. His silence may drive us to despair because we fail to make sense of a love that is economical with words. Psalm 83 begins thus: 'O God, do not keep silence; do not hold thy peace or be still, O God!' King David's cry was no less poignant: 'To thee, O Lord, I call; my rock, be not deaf to me lest, if thou be silent to me, I become like those who go down to the Pit. Hear the voice of my supplication, as I cry to thee for help, as I lift up my hand toward thy most holy sanctuary' (Psalm 28:1-2). And even Jesus gave vent to his sense of abandonment on the cross: 'My God, my God, why hast thou forsaken me?' (Matthew 27:46). And the psalmist continues: 'O my God, I cry by day, but thou dost not answer, and by bight, but find no rest... In thee our fathers trusted; they trusted and thou didst deliver them. To thee they cried, and were saved; in thee they trusted, and were not disappointed' (Psalm 22:3,5-6).

Sound and silence alternate in prayer. This dialogue with God is full of possibilities, and we conduct it in the manner which we consider best, moving from the recitation of formulae to the carrying out of our duties. This transition constitutes the more difficult but also the more valid part of prayer. When you begin the day with a prayer to God it is like throwing open the door of your house and letting in the light; and when you pray at the end of the day you are closing it with the seal of that day's portion of work and life.

Someone might ask: Why are we so bad at praying? Perhaps it has to do with our modern way of life. Today we are afflicted with so many ills, the most puzzling among them being restlessness, which in turn constantly drives us to look for a refuge for our spirit. The search for freedom from this torment of the spirit finally leads us to God.

No one should expect God to act as a therapist. A relationship would be justified only when it is based on love and not on our need for some medicine to cure our ills. Yet God as therapist is taken for granted by many people. As Fulton Sheen wrote in his *Peace of Soul,* in former times people were worried about the things of the spirit while today our concerns are strictly material. Our preoccupations tend to be economic security, health, wealth, glamour, sex. The problem really has to be dealt with quite radically at the physical and psychological levels simultaneously.

Thus for instance the Book of Job confronts the question of anxiety presented in the form of ills and disasters. The *Confessions* of St Augustine treats of the complexities of a disquieted spirit. Pascal's *Pensées* presents a depressed and vacillating human being who, bored by the tedium of his own existence, is on the quest for a utopian happiness. To quote Fulton Sheen again, all of us suffer from an anxiety complex because we possess the potential to be saints or sinners. We can choose either prayer or indifference, either God who offers love or an idol who holds out no prospects, either peace of soul or contemporary restlessness. What then is the right thing to do in order to find true happiness? Does the valley of Shangrila really exist? Is peace of soul something that can be attained by all, whether believers or not? The answers to all such questions depend on the particular temperament and cultural background of each individual.

The human psyche is a complex and delicate mechanism, unique to each person and receptive to stimuli similar to electronic waves which defy classification. Our state of mind is thus governed by our psychological disposition which might fluctuate from the good to the bad, the indifferent or the active. Prayer is a means of shaking off the temptation to do little or nothing, or to be too active or to do evil. Then prayer becomes a therapy which will pave the way for equilibrium of the spirit. Prayer frees us from the sense of being lost in modern society and makes our existential hopes come true. Prayer is meditation, colloquy, praise, exultation, faith. Prayer is a fabric woven from words and lengths of silence. Word and silence. The weight of meaning of these two terms is not lost on the professionals in the world of mass media. The main problem of every responsible journalist is perhaps how to make sensible use of the opportunities offered by word and silence.

Silence is a powerful tool in dealing with polemics and long-winded speeches. On the other hand, it becomes negative when used to evade questions. It is fine as reflection, but dangerous as refusal. Taken in its religious sense, silence gives a special meaning to prayer.

Words are a most powerful weapon when used with discretion. They give coherence to thoughts, and expression to sentiments. In the religious context, words underline a predisposition to the theological virtues of faith, hope and charity. Of these, the love of neighbour as well as the stranger is the fullest expression of the good. In dialogue we are encouraged to reach out to others, which is true charity or love. When words correspond to a sentiment, they can quicken the faculties of the mind. When words are empty they become complacent, repetitive, tiresome. They become dead ends.

In his *Conversations with Paul VI,* Jean Guitton has a passage on the word as dialogue: 'To tell the truth, it is difficult to have a dialogue. In fact, several dialogues of Plato are fictitious as they are but duets composed of monologues. Dialogue presupposes that you listen to the other. The word listen has to be understood in its divine dimension. The Boy Jesus listening to the teachers. The Risen Lord listening to the two disciples on the road to Emmaus. Man who listens to God's revelation. God who listens to man's prayer. Hence we must listen in the hope that the point of view of the speaker may enrich our thought, broaden our minds, purify our hearts, deepen our insights, elevate our spirits. An objector, an interloper, a critic are all blessings in disguise. Every objection contains a portion of truth. It forces us to clarify our thought, saving us from confusion and making our opinion lucid and objective. Dialogue is a joint exercise of listening to the truth and accepting it.'

In his message to the World Communication Day in 1980, Pope John Paul II said: 'May journalists be conscious of the enormous power of their work whether for good or evil and never betray themselves or their profession.' The pope's prayer is even more topical today with the amazing developments in printing and electronics. Now news is drowned in the restless sea of entertainment. We are indeed witnessing the death of straight and objective information. It is the hour of triumph for trash television.

'Judge not, that you be not judged. For with the judgement you pronounce you will be judged, and the measure you give will be the measure you get' (Matthew 7:1-2). No one can set himself up as the judge of others. This is especially true within the same profession. But occasionally, in blatant violation of the journalistic code of conduct, there breaks out a rash of hatred and vilification of our profession. This happens, for example, when people try to cover up or justify a wrong course of action purely out of loyalty to their own profession. It can also happen when the news is hyped and thrust upon the public in order to give the impression that they are themselves the protagonists of the story. The brashness of words and images hardly ever corresponds to the truth. On the contrary, sensationalism without any moral qualms is a slap in the face to true journalistic responsibility. The dividing line between right and wrong becomes fuzzy because of the shift in morals which is on the whole supported by the media. The majority of people in the media are usually the first to advocate total permissiveness – they are also the first to indulge in hypocritical denunciation of social evils. True, to generalise is to risk being less objective. But it is not possible to ignore this widespread trend which leads to moral as well as cultural decadence. It is not my intention to hurl accusations at the profession to which I belong; I have neither the authority nor the qualifications of a censor. I hope, if anything, to draw attention to the words addressed by the pope on the occasion of the World Day of Social Communications 1989. Quoting one of the post-conciliar documents, *Communio et Progressio,* he asked members of the mass media to assist the Church in presenting itself to the modern world, in promoting internal dialogue, in making it aware of the thinking of modern men and women, so that the Church would be able to conduct relevant discussions on the grave problems that trouble humanity.

Prayer, in the form of journalistic service, is a good medicine: 'For everything there is a season, and a time for every matter under heaven... A time to keep silence, and a time to speak' (Ecclesiastes 3:1,7). In silence and in speech, we turn to our Father who listens and speaks in silence.

Aramaic

אבונן

דבשמיא
יתקדש שמך
תיתי מלכותך
יהי צביתך היכמא
ורשמיא אף בארעא
הב כן לחמא
דסונקנן יומנא ושבוק
לן חובינן היכמא
ראף אנן שבקן לחיובינן
ולא תעילן
לניסיונא אלא נצן
מן באישתא
אמן

Our Father

What we read in childhood and adolescence remains more vivid in our minds than all the ideas we pick up in later life. How can one forget that powerful page in Victor Hugo's *The Man Who Laughs* which gives an eye-witness account of the death of some people who were shipwrecked? Buffeted between reef and surf, taking in water on every side, the vessel *Matutina* is totally at the mercy of the waves. The crew and the passengers see the end approaching and they are numbed by fear. 'Then, at that moment of despair, they heard the voice of the doctor who said, "Let us pray." They all went down on their knees. They had only a few minutes left. The doctor made the sign of the cross and spoke in a loud voice while under his feet he could feel the beginning of that almost imperceptible tilt which marks the moment when a wreck starts sinking. He began: "Pater noster qui es in coelis." The provençal echoed in French: "Notre Père qui êtes aux cieux." The Irishman repeated in Gaelic which the Basque woman could understand: "Ar nathair ata ar neamh." The doctor continued: "Sanctificetur nomen tuum." "Que votre nome soit sanctifié," said the provençal. "Naomhthar hainm," the Irishman said. Water had reached the shoulders of the kneeling figures. "Adveniat regnum tuum," continued the doctor. "Que votre règne arrive," said the provençal. "Tigeadh do rioghachd," said the Irishman. Then the doctor resumed: "Fiat voluntas tua." "Que votre volonté soit faite," the provençal said in a faltering voice. And the Irishman and the Basque woman cried: "Deuntar do thail ar an Hhalàmb!" "Sicut in coelo et in terra," said the doctor. No voice rose in reply. He lowered his eyes. All the heads were under the water. No one had stood up. They had drowned kneeling.'

I still recall vividly the dramatic quality of that account and the persuasive power of that invocation which dispelled the fear of imminent death.

The universality of this prayer is illustrated in a real-life incident. It happened many years ago – I have no idea exactly when or where – a hundred wise men had met to discuss the essential matters of the world. They came from far countries, spoke different languages, possessed knowledge in diverse fields, and evaluated the happenings of the world according to their contrasting mentalities. None of them would willingly concede that the others were right. Then one of them made this suggestion: 'Since we have failed to reach any agreement, let us seek inspiration through a prayer.' Some took offence, some were perplexed, but the majority agreed. Then another problem arose. Which prayer? Their differences of opinion threatened to resurface until the original proposer told them that there was a prayer, perhaps the only one in the world, which would be acceptable to an adherent of any religion – the Our Father. This episode is a lesson that teaches us the possibilities for mutual understanding among differing persons when there exists even a minimum of goodwill.

That lesson was proved right again on 27 October 1986 at Assisi in Italy, where Christians, Muslims, Jews, Buddhists and followers of many other religions were gathered in praise and adoration of God the Creator of the universe. Pope John Paul II began the prayer: 'Eternal Father and Lord of Peace, hear us on this day in Christ Jesus, your Eternal Son.' He was followed by the Methodist pastor, Emilio Castro, Secretary of the Ecumenical Council of Churches: 'Let us seek reconciliation so that we may become credible.' Then the Dalai Lama: 'Peace begins within us.' And Rabbi Elio Toaff: 'A dialogue is possible on the great themes of humanity: peace, justice, morality.' In his turn, the Muslim leader Khaled Fuad Allam said: 'The experience of dialogue is a radical experience because it forces us to renounce our prejudices against others.' The fact that the divisions are still there does not matter; what is important is that the world religious leaders abandoned their old mental attitude of opposition for the sake of unity of spirit – at least once in their life.

The recitation of the Lord's Prayer paves the way to unity. For it is a prayer which is complete in every way and easily adaptable for any monotheistic religion. For the Christians this prayer constitutes – as affirmed right at the beginning of the third century by the brilliant writer Tertullian – 'a true synthesis of the Gospel.' And today also this prayer is perfectly suited for those who work in the media of social communication – the world of ambitions, jealousy, scandals, lies, delusions, where there is little regard for truth or morality. No wonder Dante chose to meditate on the Lord's Prayer during his passage through purgatory. Which group is more guilty of the sin of pride than the journalists? Which group is more boastful and conceited than the press persons? And who is more adept at twisting words than those who work in the mass media? A re-reading of this universal prayer thus gives us yet another chance to meditate on the weaknesses of the modern world and on its possible transformation.

The Lord's Prayer teaches us many things. Consider, for example, the newspaper industry which is closely linked with the world of entertainment through advertising. You soon discover a baffling mixture of persons and motives. Everyone is eager to succeed – even if it means selling their talents short or ditching their friends. It is natural that we should try to stand out from the greyness of anonymity – the usual excuse! – but we never pause to analyse our strengths and weaknesses, taking it for granted that we are the best. Presumption, which at times borders on haughtiness, seems to be the trademark of the journalistic profession. Small wonder. In the business of self-promotion how can anyone refrain from blowing up the self? Have you ever seen anyone foolish enough to efface themselves by underrating or even hiding altogether the fruit of their labours? No one who would be so foolish could be a journalist – at least not according to the stereotype image. They would risk being cold shouldered in the ruthless world of the mass media which applauds those who show initiative but which, on the other hand, fights shy of committment and professional responsibility.

In difficult moments I turn to God the Father because I lack the confidence to have direct recourse to the Spirit for help. In former times they used to debate whether God had made man in his image or whether man had made God conform to his own mental picture. This question can only be resolved by contrasting God's perfection (the Infinite) with man's imperfection (the finite). Through this process I come upon a whole range of concepts which are in themselves well-meaning, at times arrogant, and often inadequate.

I ask God the Father for forgiveness. I know only too well my faults that will accompany me to the grave. How often I have tried to shake off my pride. I think I have failed but I still hope to change my attitude towards others – my colleagues in the office as well as my readers and the public at large who follow radio and television programmes. Will I get another chance for change?

I believe there is some special way for changing our lives, for deepening our personal commitment to the ethics of our profession. I recall reading somewhere this striking sentence: 'This society is atheistic not because it does not love God – it is atheistic because it does not love humanity.' For those who work in the sphere of social communication – writers, journalists, film directors, technicians, public relations officers – to love their neighbour implies a continuous search for truth. Thus, through the medium of men and women, the most special and intelligent species God created for managing our planet, we arrive at a knowledge of God. On the same analogy, the media can be an effective tool in the fight against atheism insofar as it is forgetfulness and indifference to God. On the other hand, those who misuse the means of communication are guilty of alienating from God numerous people who are influenced by papers and magazines and radio and television broadcasts.

The Church is aware of the abuse of information and entertainment by the mass media. But it is not easy to fight forces that are in pursuit of money and power to the exclusion of any spiritual objective. It is interesting to note in this context that the *Osservatore Romano*, the official paper of the Vatican, on several occasions issued warnings against certain perversions in modern society only to be branded as old-fashioned by some sections of the media, obviously because the paper clashed with vested interests. The paper has had the same experience when dealing with moral values, bioethics, social habits. I therefore begin to wonder if there really exists the type of journalist or media corporation that can resist this materialistic tendency. The ideal solution would be to train young professionals who would show respect for truth, objectivity and morality. This is not an impractical plan, especially if we seek the help of those media people who adhere to Christian principles or secular integrity.

No doubt, these three values of truth, objectivity and morality are taught. But truth does not ripen in the sun like a fruit on a tree. We have to seek it and draw attention to it: the good is shy. The mystic Simone Weil wrote: 'To love truth is to accept emptiness, and therefore death.' When applied to journalism, these words mean standing serenely, every morning, at the window of life in order to observe the little as well as the big events and report them faithfully. In other words, we must above all respect ourselves.

Objectivity demands that we should be faithful to events and give the right amount of time and space to each news item, without stressing a comment here or twisting a detail there. In other words, we must respect people and facts.

Morality has a close link with reason. According to Kant and other thinkers of the modern era, ethics is the guarantee for happiness. In our context, this link acts as a check on bad taste, the degradation of the human being, the erosion of spiritual values. To play down this connection, dismissing the argument as moralism, is nothing short of acting in bad faith. And think of the consequences, the problems in real life such an attitude creates and condones. In other words, we must respect life.

In shaping public opinion the media have well-defined responsibilities which must never be shirked. The public also has a duty to use discretion and judgement in their choice of papers and programmes. Thus the question of God is inseparable from the affairs of the world.

دُعا

اے ہمارے باپ تو جو آسمان پر ہے تیرا نام پاک مانا جائے ● تیری بادشاہی آئے تیری مرضی جیسی آسمان پر پوری ہوتی ہے زمین پر بھی ہو ● ہماری روز کی روٹی آج ہمیں دے ● اور جس طرح ہم نے اپنے قرضداروں کو معاف کیا ہے تو بھی ہمارے قرض ہمیں معاف کر ● اور ہمیں آزمائش میں نہ لا بلکہ برائی سے بچا کیونکہ بادشاہی اور قدرت اور جلال ہمیشہ تیرے ہی ہیں (آمین)

Sanskrit

प्रभु-वंदना

भो अस्माकं स्वर्गस्थ पितः,
तव नाम पवित्रं पूज्यतां ।
तव राज्यमायातु ।
यथा स्वर्गे तथा मेदिन्यामपि
तवेच्छा सिध्यतु ।
श्वस्तनं भक्ष्यमद्याप्यमर्भ्यं देहि ।
वयंच यथास्मदपराधिना क्षमामहे,
तथा त्वमस्माकपराधान् क्षमस्व ।
अस्मांश्च परीक्षां मा नय,
अपितु दुरात्मत उद्धर ।
तथास्तु ।

Who art in heaven

Jesus liked to retreat to lonely places in order to pray undisturbed. Deserts, hilltops, woods, riverbanks – he loved such spots, preferably at dawn, at dusk or during the night. Bowing, kneeling or prostrated, he would raise his eyes to his Father who is in heaven. Whenever we are alone with nature we have a yearning to commune with God. This is why throughout the centuries holy men and women have withdrawn to the solitude of the mountains and the seas. And even people who are totally immersed in their work are anxious to reduce to the minimum the bustle around them. I am thinking of the artisans of the past and the intellectuals of today.

But it is a completely different story when we come to the factories where the assembly lines have become veritable chains of the workers whose enervating drudgery is a violation of human dignity. Our society is able to depreciate creativity with the excuse of machines and circumstances that restrict freedom of expression. I think of those who work in radio and television, in the claustrophobic little editing rooms, in work places which take their toll on the body and militate against the equation of work equals prayer.

To those who work in the media heaven seems hopelessly far. The realm of God is light years away. The kingdom of the Spirit is surrounded by a wall without gates. This incapacity to communicate stems from the current all-consuming passion for power and money. Yet there is a key to the door of this *non-place,* this *utopia,* this antithesis of the world. It is a simple key. Love. Just as love did not allow God to remain alone (as Thomas Aquinas wrote), so human beings can be with God through love, the treasure of our hearts. Obviously, not a few treasures are sought after and highly esteemed. But these are earthly treasures.

The distinction is important. Jesus himself has taught us to discriminate between the things of the world and those of heaven. At the Last Supper, Jesus' discourse to the disciples had a message of great ecumenical import. Addressing the Father, he said: 'I have manifested thy name to the men whom thou gavest me out of the world... I am no more in the world... Keep them in thy name that they may be one... Sanctify them in the truth' (John 17:6,11,17). A universal message understood and handed down through the centuries by a minority for a minority. This minority now has the responsibility of defining work as right and duty. The two terms are closely linked. For we aspire to serve the community through our work and at the same time we are expected to do our jobs conscientiously.

Do the media people somehow form part of this minority? Perhaps I am a pessimist and I have my doubts, for it seems to me that they are not quite familiar with heaven. Perhaps they do not spend enough time thinking about heaven. They do not realise that heaven is everywhere, in us, in the lowliest as well as in the highest, in those who believe and in those who oppose the faith. Some years ago, while commenting on the Lord's Prayer, an Italian priest drew a comparison between heaven and a prison he had just visited: 'Heaven is each soul.

We have perhaps lost this sense of the divine in each creature which will put up such a brave fight against evil that it is transformed into a gleam of light. And it is here, in this heaven, that you sometimes see a hurricane.'

This hurricane, this struggle, we in the media world too often observe with the typical indifference of non-participants. Words become like bricks that bruise and do not build. Closed within our own selfishness, we are more concerned about the parameters of profits just as we are more interested in criticising the achievements of others. Being in love with our own way of talking and writing, we fuss over aesthetic niceties rather than gain a deeper understanding of news and its concrete and practical presentation.

We are too concerned with theoretical construction. Sometimes I feel that we are doing what Lazaro Ludovico Zamenhof did when he invented Esperanto, the language which is as technically perfect and easy to understand as it is alien and contrary to any particular culture. Or perhaps we are no less unrealistic than the Hindu religion which tries to combine specific principles of individuals and groups into a collective of sects with nothing in common but vague geographical boundaries and a literary language (Sanskrit) now known to not more than five thousand scholars and students. By the same analogy, we create a product which is print and screen perfect, but which is accessible only to a restricted number. The end result is artificial.

Instead, there is nothing artificial at all in the work of missionaries anywhere, especially in India which has always been an ideal place for spiritual conquests. Forty odd years ago, when India became independent, there began the exodus of foreign missionaries due to a deliberate government policy. Today very few are allowed to stay. It could have been the end of an epoch, but it turned out to be the dawn of a new religious era for the land that was evangelised by St Thomas the Apostle. New indigenous communities have sprung up in many places, vocations have multiplied, the faith has found a new vigour, and young people have discovered a joyous way of freeing themselves from caste and social ostracism. Today the Indian Church is self-sufficient and sends its priests and sisters to do missionary work in other parts of the world. It is a lesson that highlights the possibility for every local Church – especially in the Third World – to stand on its own feet.

Churches outside Europe have to adapt to different rites and attitudes. It is only by steeping ourselves in their cultures that we will be able to understand the religious spirit of the Indians, the Africans, the Chinese or the Americans. The fault, as I see it, of the experts in religious journalism lies in interpreting every phenomenon within the terms of reference of the Church officials in the Vatican. It should not be so. I totally agree with what I read in *Cammino* (the journal of Capuchin missions, Milan 1989): 'What is striking about the Catholic Church in India is its capacity to adapt itself to every need where doctrine becomes word, word becomes silence, and action when it is necessary to act against poverty and death. This explains the great esteem in India for the Church as an institution with large material resources and as companion in life.' Mother Teresa of Calcutta always makes headlines, but the Third World can offer any number of similar cases – seeds that prepare the harvest in the fields.

It is action, not rhetoric, that bears fruit. This was also what a great spirit of our age, Mahatma Gandhi, used to counsel: 'A prayer without words is better than many words without prayer.'

Hindi

प्रभु की विनती

हे हमारे पिता जो स्वर्ग में है ।
तेरा नाम पवित्र किया जाये ।
तेरा राज्य आये ।
तेरी इच्छा जैसे स्वर्ग में
वैसे पृथ्वी पर भी पूरी हो ।
हमारा प्रतिदिन का आहार
आज हमें दे,
और हमारे अपराध हमें क्षमा कर,
जैसे हम भी अपने अपराधियों को
क्षमा करते हैं,
और हमको परीक्षा में न डाल,
परन्तु बुराई से बचा ।
आमेन ।

Hallowed
be thy name

When Jesus taught his disciples the prayer which is the quintessence of his teaching, he must have had in his mind echoes of the chanting of the *Qaddish:* 'The name of the Lord be praised and hallowed in the world he created according to his will. May he establish his kingdom in your life and in the life of Israel and its generations. Amen. Blessed be the name of the Lord on earth and in eternity. The name of the Holy One be blessed, praised, honoured, exalted, magnified and glorified... May he be blessed beyond all blessing and all hymning, beyond all praise and all joy in this world. May all the prayers and supplications of the entire people of Israel find acceptance in the presence of their Father who is in heaven. Amen. Blessed be the name of the Lord, now and for ever. The great peace of heaven and earth be upon us and upon all Israel.

Amen. All help comes to me from God who made heaven and earth. May the maker of peace in heaven bring peace to us and to all Israel. And all say: Amen.'

The third verse of the Our Father is practically the same as the opening formula of the *Qaddish,* and the Jewish-Aramaic roots of both prayers are not in question. But what is the correct interpretation of the verse 'hallowed be thy name'? Let glory be rendered to the Lord's name? Or may the Father's name be worthy of blessing? Philologically, the argument could be a protracted one indeed. In practice, however, it would be sufficient to think of an act of adoration, respect, acknowledgement, homage.

This was precisely what Jesus had in mind: to give a clear idea of the relationship between us and God. There have been many attempts to describe God's love for us. A more recent example is a novel called *The Man from Nazareth* which depicts the life of Jesus. Here is an extract from it:

The sky was overcast with thick dark clouds. And, all of a sudden, Jesus said, 'Let me tell you about prayer.' 'You mean,' James asked, 'you want to start praying, now?' 'Don't pray shouting out loud like the hypocrites in synagogues and at street corners. Pray instead in silence and in the secret of your hearts, for your heavenly Father is not deaf.' 'What words are we to use?' asked John. 'Words that simply ask for the things you need.' Jesus had to raise his voice to be heard above the wind. 'Here!' Simon shouted to the boatman, 'let me handle that oar.' And Jesus continued, 'Thus: Our Father in heaven, let your name be blessed. Grant us to see the coming of your kingdom. May your will be done on earth as we know it is fulfilled in heaven. Today give us the food we need for today. Forgive our wrongs as we hope to forgive the wrongs others do to us. Let our trials be neither too hard nor too many, for we are weak and brittle. And protect us from the snares of evil. These simple words are all you need. And now I think I'll sleep for a while.' 'What! With a storm brewing?' Andrew was astonished. And Jesus replied patiently, 'You must learn the art of sleeping when and where possible.' 'You can rest now,' said John, 'we'll keep watch for you.'

This was yet another beautiful lesson Jesus taught us. The manager of a factory or the director of a company should know how to balance his or her physical and intellectual energies through the alternation of work and rest. But the lesson is little understood by our society which has become restless with the stress of work which is supposed to lead to success, money and power.

Everyone wants to play manager. They may have nothing to show for it, but the important thing – as the saying goes – is to get in on the act, never mind the consequences. And many enter this race. The information industry has opened up new patches for profit making. The range is wide indeed. In this sector the lean cows of Pharaoh had appeared first. Now it seems to be the time of the fat cows. The industry is looking good with its thousand and one political and commercial outlets which have perfected the art of hiding the profits and balancing the books.

It is these manipulators of the media who should pay special heed to Jesus' invocation: 'Hallowed be thy name.' During his public life Jesus was fond of talking directly to the people in very simple language. He often had recourse to parables and fables, knowing fully well that he was dealing with humble folks without the benefit of education as we understand it today. To the crowds he must have spoken in the dialect of Samaria or Galilee, while with the teachers he might have used Aramaic and with the Roman rulers probably Latin. Jesus also took delight in spending time in the synagogue to read and explain the scriptures. One of the evangelists, for example, has recorded: 'And he came to Nazareth... And he stood up to read... And he closed the book, and gave it back to the attendant, and sat down' (Luke 4:16-20).

Jesus willingly preached, taught, prophesied, admonished, healed and journeyed. But he never wrote. It seems he took no interest in the art of writing. The disciples have recorded only one instance where Jesus actually wrote something – in the sand. And what he wrote vanished without a trace while his words passed on to us through the gospels have endured. Let us read again that passage: 'The scribes and the Pharisees brought a woman who had been caught in adultery... "Now in the law

Moses commanded us to stone such. What do you say about her?" This they said to test him... Jesus bent down and wrote with his finger on the ground... "Let him who is without sin among you be the first to throw a stone at her." And once more he bent down and wrote with his finger on the ground' (John 8:3-8).

If Jesus were to write today how much time he would need to spend at the word processor or the computer. How often he would be forced to intervene in order to keep banks and businesses on the straight and narrow. How many times he would have to explain the optimum link between money and conscience.

The chapter on social ethics has yet to be written in the Christian sense. However, it is comforting to know that some business schools in Britain have introduced such principles into their curriculum, meeting with both approval and success.

Hallowed be thy name. Not enough attention is paid to this verse. Essentially to hallow means to practise virtue (in its widest sense) and to do good so that the targeted work output is reached without compromising one's conscience. I think the Lord won't at all mind if the praise of his name is interrupted for the sake of the spiritual glorification of man. The respect for human dignity has to withstand various tests. The test of products and factors that form the character of the individual and the society is not least among them.

French

Notre Père

qui es aux cieux
que ton nom soit sanctifié;
que ton règne vienne;
que ta volonté soit faite
sur la terre
comme au ciel.
Donne-nous aujourd'hui notre pain
de ce jour;
pardonne-nous nos offenses
comme nous pardonnons aussi à
ceux
qui nous ont offensés
et ne nous soumets pas à la
tentation;
mais délivre nous du mal.
Amen.

Thy kingdom come

In his book *Man and the State* Jacques
Maritain wrote: 'In times of crisis, change
and renewal, the role of the prophets of the
people truly comes to the fore. I think of the
fathers of the French Revolution, the
architects of the American Constitution, the
leaders of the Italian Risorgimento, and the
fighters for Irish Independence. I also think
of Mahatma Gandhi, the pioneers of Trade
Unionism and the trail blazers of the
Workers Movement. The first task of such
inspired leaders is to fire the imagination of
the people.'

These prophets and social reformers also
had a vision which took them beyond their
local and national boundaries to the whole
of humanity. They were certain that there
was no contradiction between social aspirations and moral imperatives.

I am not a politician but right from my

youth I have always taken an interest in politics. Wanting to go from theory to practice, I even started a magazine. It was published solely through my personal savings and the help of my friends. A mere publishing trifle. But to us it was an amazing means of announcing our radical message to the whole world. Thirty years have gone by, and nothing has changed – if anything, things have got worse.

I like politics, but I don't care for party politics and profiteering. So I keep aloof from the complexities of the day to day running of the country. At one time there was open and unrelenting war over ideologies, not over power and corruption. Then one had a few bones broken in public and honest fights, but nobody shot defenceless people in the back or, still less, plotted the downfall of those who dared to think for themselves and swam against the current.

Perhaps I should not shut myself in, taking refuge in the past. According to Charles Peguy, the soul is not to be preserved like a private treasure, but to be generously distributed like a public fund even at the risk of making mistakes. I have thus found that there can be a free vote for Christians. We need not show allegiance to the same party always. We should be free to switch our support to a party with the best political and ethical credentials. In other words, a party with the wrong policies cannot expect to win votes by adopting a religious label. In politics it is easy to make mistakes, but it is the good intentions and the right objectives that matter. Let us hope – and here I repeat a quote from Emmanuel Mounier's *The agony of Christianity* – that 'when a Christian makes a mistake, at least let it be made with a dash of nobleness, audacity, challenge, adventure, passion'. Regrettably, however, we have to admit that some politicians with a Christian orientation prefer to limit themselves to the parochial, avoiding challenge and courageous action. When confronted by an aggressive adversary, they become accommodating and, fearing public criticism and loss of popularity, they abdicate their role as elected representatives of the people.

But it would be blasphemous to think that the expression 'thy kingdom come' means that God is going to come down and establish a dictatorship on earth. Monsignor Giuseppe Riciotti shows how this verse does not signify a political evolution, which perhaps made sense to the Roman (pagan) mind but was totally alien to the Jewish (religious) way of thinking. For the teaching of Jesus was aimed at eliminating the tension between two cultures by removing the scandal of the Pharisees and the distrust of the Romans.

In his book *The hidden years of Jesus* Robert Aron says that Jesus surmounted the opposition between the old and the new through the audacious departure of speaking without referring to this or that Talmudist. Instead he adopted as his own certain strands in the thinking of the teachers so that he enjoyed a spiritual independence which not even Moses had attained. This becomes evident from the fact that Jesus spoke in the name of God, his Father, discarding tradition and stressing a personal link with the Creator. This style was disconcerting to the mentality of the age and fascinating to future generations.

Thus we see that it is possible for any political debate to be permeated with the leaven of the sacred. Ernest Renan, author of the controversial *Life of Jesus*, commenting on the Our Father, remarked how

Jesus repeatedly stressed that the heavenly Father knows our needs better than we do and to ask him for the wrong thing is almost an insult. 'And in praying do not heap up empty phrases as the Gentiles do; for they think that they will be heard for their many words. Do not be like them, for your Father knows what you need before you ask him' (Matthew 6:7-8). This is valid for the individual, the community, the world.

Let me conclude with the words of Paul VI, who gave us this counsel: 'Politics is a calling – albeit not exclusive – that demands the Christian commitment to serve others' (*Octogesima Adveniens*). When therefore we say 'thy kingdom come' we should bear in mind these words of the pope since, as Christian journalists, we are called to build a society that will respect the teaching of Christ.

Spanish

Padre nuestro

que estás en el cielo,
santificado sea tu Nombre;
venga tu reino;
hágase tu voluntad
en la tierra
como en el cielo;
da nos hoy nuestro pan de cada
  día;
perdona nuestra ofensas,
como también nosotros
  perdonamos
a los que nos ofenden;
no nos dejes caer en tentación,
y líbranos del mal.
Amen.

Thy will be done

What is meant by obedience to God's will? Is it the so-called Christian resignation or is it a specific act of trust? Why should God, who is all-powerful, forgo the means to make his will respected and rely on the voluntary submission of human beings? Or, what does divine sovereignty consist in?

For answers to such questions we must turn to the early commentators on the Lord's Prayer. Cyprian and Augustine both give an anthropological nature to God's will: in man heaven is the spirit, the earth his body, the reason for conforming to a superior will being for man a moral imperative to live with 'good will' – implying good behaviour, sensible speech, modest dress, psychological balance, religious steadfastness. All this in order to comply with the words of Jesus: 'You shall love the Lord your God with all your heart... You shall love your neighbour as yourself' (Matthew 22:37,39). For the media persons these words, which sum up the two great commandments, are condensed into the expression 'search for truth'.

Truth constitutes a phoneme as fascinating as it is utopian. Truth presents a thousand different faces, making it extremely difficult to discern the right one for the right moment. Conscience alone is capable of such discernment for, according to St Thomas Aquinas, truth is to be found in the human heart. We read in his *On the True Religion:* 'Do not exit, return to your own self. It is in the interior man that truth has its dwelling. And if you find that truth is inconstant in your heart, then transcend yourself.' Truth is proclaimed from roof tops since it alone sets us really free, as St John tells us in his gospel. So we carry on our shoulders a tremendous responsibility and our conscience is the guide in our search for truth.

'I live yet I do not live, and the life I hope for is so sublime that I die because I am not dying.' Thus wrote St Teresa of Avila in *The Interior Castle,* explaining how the prayer to the Father lends itself to the particular needs of each individual because in a few words it encompasses all that can be said and how, possessing this prayer, you need no other book. This Carmelite reformer does not usually find many readers among media people in spite of all the talk about feminism and equality of the sexes in Church and society. Which is a pity. For the teaching of this woman contains the most basic elements that invite you to orient your personal life in keeping with God's image which reflects, in the Our Father, the same existential itinerary of humanity.

Let us return to the concept of truth. What does truth mean to a journalist? Above all, it is a question of professional integrity. To tell the truth through a job properly done. This can be elaborated in three points.

First, information is the right of a democratic society. The journalist is, of course, free to tap sources of information and offer analyses and opinions. But the privacy of the individual has to be safeguarded at every stage of any assignment.

Secondly, it follows logically that a journalist should only give correct information, with the right space and balance in order not to distort its sense and scale. A journalist should avoid plagiarism, calumny and defamation, resisting any glorification of crime or justification of abnormal or degrading practices. Nor must a journalist accept invitations to contribute to publications that are racist, pornographic, sadistic or in any other way offensive to human dignity.

Thirdly, journalists must respect the right of readers, listeners and viewers to be free to form a true and informed opinion of events with the help of news reports that are unambiguous and unbiased by particular ideologies. People have a right to protect their reputation. It is therefore unethical to publicise facts and circumstances that would violate the privacy of the individual. Hence it is important to avoid scandalous insinuations and accusations for reasons of financial gain, personal grudge or sheer social titillation.

Let us recall the advice St Ignatius Loyola gave to some of his followers in a mission field: 'It is better to preach the Catholic faith, bear witness to it and establish it quietly than to cause clamour by persecuting the heretics, who might become more obstinate if they notice that you are openly preaching against them; but hearing the truths to the contrary, they might perhaps be converted. Therefore do all things with Christian charity and gentleness, neither offending nor rejecting anyone.' This is sound work ethics, not pastoral cunning.

Pay nosso

que estaes n'o ceo,
sanctificado seja o vosso nome;
venha a nòs o vosso reyno.
Seja feita a vossa vontade
assim n'a terra
como n'o ceo.
O pão nosso de cada dia nos day
    hoje.
Perdonainos nossas dividas,
assim como nos perdoamos aos
    nossos devedores.
E não nos deixeis cahir em
    tantaçaõ;
mai livrainos do mal.
Amen.

On earth

Wanting to relax, I decide to read some poetry. So I open the bible and find King David who sings: 'Come, O sons, listen to me, I will teach you the fear of the Lord... Keep your tongue from evil, and your lips from speaking deceit.' (Psalm 34:11,13). And further on he returns to the same theme: 'Set a guard over my mouth, O Lord, keep watch over the door of my lips! Incline not my heart to any evil' (Psalm 141:3-4).

The psalms are 'praises' in the Hebrew way of thinking and 'hymns to be sung to the accompaniment of music', as the Greeks understand them. If I may borrow the words of John Calvin, the psalms penetrate and reveal the soul most accurately. They are songs which can be sung by anyone, whether they are believers or not. In fact, those who do not believe may gain more from the psalms because they are in most need of realising that there exists a God of 'those without God' – a God who worries them with thoughts, tortures them with existential angst, unsettles them with doubts, torments them with love.

Nietzsche insisted that he rid himself of the problem by declaring that God was dead. The German philosopher still has a large following. To a great extent, it consists of the mughals of the media industry which continually churns out facts and figures of a defeated society, pandering to the morbidity of every individual and broadcasting the false glamour of evil. Papers that specialise in printing scandalous stories claim that they do it merely to stay alive – the competition is so stiff! Such justification obviously has no moral grounds whatever. The truth of the matter is that their concern is to make money. What future in terms of freedom and responsibility is there for a press whose sole concern is circulation and popularity rating?

Often, those who work in the media do not wish to admit that human life is transitory, that the media themselves are ephemeral or that the life span of a paper is as short as a little sigh. It is the fate of all earthly things. Only in heaven will we find eternity.

Signs of the times. This is an expression used in all sorts of contexts. Used by Jesus, this phrase points to the various stages of our journey into the future. However, a warning must be sounded: even our faith can be caught up in the confusion of the times and we may find it hard to keep on the right track. The only refuge for the restlessness of this world is to be found in Christianity, which is a religion of hope.

Experts warn that our society cannot last much longer due to over-population, depletion of energy sources, pollution and nuclear proliferation. In this predicament, what is the message from Christ? He censures those who do not heed his teaching, branding them as 'hypocrites'. He was speaking to his contemporaries, but his message is valid for all ages. His mandate is to apply ethical standards in the use of science and technology so that they may yield spiritual as well as material benefits. Once again we see the enormous responsibility of those who work in the mass media.

I came across this passage in Rudolf Schnackenburg's book *Reading the Signs of the Times:* 'For the Christian there are causes that are deeper than the events of this world; and there are other signs which disclose themselves to the eye of faith. Then there is the power of evil which is capable of reducing to nothing even the best of intentions. However, the Christian can also recognise the forces of good which have been released in the world by Jesus. It is this hope that constantly spurs us into action.' May this same hope inspire Christian workers in the media.

In the media, everything is a team effort. Each one has to show moral responsibility, integrity of work, respect for people, propriety of means employed. Responsibility also raises the question of professional competence not as an end in itself, but with reference to the evolution of social needs and behaviour and culture in general. In other words, our professional competence has a direct bearing on the life of society. The emphasis then shifts to moral principles which the communicator must always take into account.

For those who take their faith seriously, what matters most is respect for others as individuals, whether weak or strong. Such respect is then extended to the whole community, for ultimately a message is never meant solely for the individual but for society as a whole.

Romano Guardini – the Italian-born thinker and writer in German – wrote that our language is shaped by the way our reason develops and our being attains complete union with God. Guardini believed that our experience (*Erlebnis*) is transformed into virtue when it is an assertion of rational and moral values. Invocation, prayer, hope – these are some of the means for delving into the recesses of the soul. Finally the soul is led into the realm of serenity which can justly be qualified as sacred because it is closely linked to the witness of faith and freedom. (Guardini himself suffered under Nazi persecution.)

Indeed, praying for oneself and for others is a proper witness to freedom. Therefore, as Christians and as workers in the communications media, we cannot ignore the exhortation of Pope John Paul II: 'Whenever you report on the life and activity of the Church, strive to capture the true spiritual driving force of its thought and action. And the Church, on its part, will take note of the testimony of journalists on the needs and aspirations of the world' (Address to the International Press, 21 October 1978). And, precisely on account of our Christian faith, we must ensure that our professional service rises above daily routine by virtue of its spiritual dimension.

It then becomes simply a question of opening the Bible when we are troubled by doubts and we shall find meaning to our life on earth. I am reminded of a profound remark made by the theologian Adolf von Harnack: 'There is no substitute for the gospel.' The suffering and anxiety of the Old Testament give way in the gospels to the blessings of a paradisiacal future which can become a present reality in our midst, on earth, well before we reach heaven.

Italian

Padre nostro

che sei nei cieli,
sia santificato il tuo nome,
venga il tuo regno,
sia fatta la tua volontà,
   come in cielo, così in terra.
Dacci oggi il nostro pane
   quotidiano,
e rimetti a noi i nostri debiti,
   come noi li rimettiamo ai
   nostri debitori;
e non c'indurre in tentazione,
ma liberaci dal male.
Amen.

German

Vater unser

im Himmel,
geheiligt werde dein Name.
Dein Reich komme.
Dein Wille geschehe
wie im Himmel
so auf Erden.
Unser tägliches Brot gib uns
   heute.
Und vergib uns unsere Schuld,
wie auch wir vergeben unsern
   Schuldigern.
Und führe uns nicht in
   Versuchung,
sondern erlöse uns von dem
   Bösen.
Amen.

As it is in heaven

Working in radio or television is not easy. Most people think otherwise and plunge in with disastrous results. They fail to appreciate that in the shaping of public opinion radio and television have the edge over any other means of communication. If a transmission makes a positive cultural contribution, fine. But the problem is that in the majority of cases radio and television programmes only accelerate the deterioration of social and moral behaviour. This is obviously not done on purpose. It is due to superficiality or the fear on the part of controllers and producers who do not want to look unfashionable. Another factor to blame is the inherently mistaken attitude of many media persons who are quite happy with the repetitiveness of themes and the banality of language.

There is little change in the schedule. In

politics turns and times are strictly observed according to custom and protocol. In the media holiday reports, plays, news conferences and other items succeed one another in the monotonous journalistic calendar with such regularity that the same script could be used year after year. In trade union disputes the tendency is to report with seeming impartiality, justifying every initiative by recognised groups and branding all others as cowboy cliques. In sports the practice is to build up personalities and teams into myths who, poor devils, bite the dust with the first sign of failure. In entertainment even the slightest hint of criticism is avoided on the assumption that the stars are inviolable and that the bovine public accepts anything.

From time to time some intellectual or other makes a half-hearted gesture of protest, but no more. Everyone likes to be invited to the broadcasting studios – it is unwise to risk being excluded.

It looks as if nothing short of a miracle can change the present state of affairs in the media world. The teaching of the Church has a value which is valid everywhere and at all times, and therefore in the case of our very sophisticated means it should not be difficult to apply the advice of St Paul: 'Whatever a man sows, that he will reap. For he who sows to his own flesh will from the flesh reap corruption; but he who sows to the Spirit will from the Spirit reap eternal life' (Galatians 6:7-8). The warning is clear. By disseminating a lifestyle dominated exclusively by material values, religious media persons risk involvement in misguided causes. Again, anxious to keep up with others, religious media services might be tempted to follow the fad of 'covering' anything new, creating in the process considerable confusion about what is happening in society.

A television company that ignores educational and religious programmes or relegates them to unpopular slots is only helping to engender distorted attitudes among the young, who in later years will repay in kind what they have received from the previous generation.

The same is true of the world of newspapers and magazines. After all, radio, television and press have a symbiotic existence. The evening news broadcasts are picked up and expanded by the following morning's papers and radio programmes. It is a case of the dog chasing its tail.

If prayer is truth, and if truth corresponds to reports in the media, then we have many 'prayers' presented to us every hour. For a true understanding of our society we should opt for a parallel or integrated analysis of what is offered by the various media services. Radio is the fastest means of information; television with its visual images is the most effective means of communication; the press completes the picture with background detail and in-depth analysis. At least, this is the theory.

Every question deserves special attention. Let us, for example, take a problem that affects the entire human race. The ecological crisis. We are destroying the earth in the name of progress. What is portentous is the genocide of the Amazonian Indians along with the destruction of the Brazilian forests. Here we are witnessing the suicide of the ancient and noble Portuguese civilisation. It is a phenomenon of profound seriousness as it threatens human life and its relationship with the rest of the universe. Christians cannot afford to ignore this ecological disaster because it involves the entire cosmos – the creation of the Father who is in heaven.

The degradation of the earth points our discussion yet again towards heaven. If we do not take good care of what God has entrusted to us, then we have no right to ask for his mercy. In the wake of the nuclear disaster at Chernobyl, Pope John Paul II warned: 'The very concept of man's relationship with the Absolute is in danger. The new technologies compel us to rediscover the foundations of the perennial moral laws and to reflect in depth on human nature, on the intrinsic value of every individual, on scientific research in its widest sense and on the significance of human actions in relation to Christ, the focus of history and the cosmos.'

As a believing Christian I try to distinguish between the medium and the message. There then arises the question of how to make my faith reflect on my work in the complex world of communication. There are several ways of doing so. And it is possible to effect change. For the better.

Polish

Ojcze nasz

któryś jest w niediesiech,
swieć sie Imie Twoje,
przyjdz Królestwo Twoje,
badz wola Twoja
jako w niebie
tak i na ziemi.
Chleba naszego powszedniego
    daj nam dzisiaj
i odpusc nam nasze winy,
jako i my odpuszczamy naszym
    winowajcom,
i nie wodz nas na pokuszenie,
ale nas zbaw ode zlego.
Amen.

Give us this day
our daily bread

Great souls have an appropriate thought for every situation. Here is one of Mahatma Gandhi's sayings: 'If we all worked to earn our bread, class distinctions would soon be abolished. The rich might be there always; but they would see themselves as administrators of resources meant for the common good.' Although Gandhi is talking about material things, the underlying spiritual significance of his words is undeniable. The same is true of the verse in the Lord's Prayer where we seek bread for the body.

The bread of life is the essence of the Christian message. Work, which is necessary for survival, is the most important need in any society. Work for obtaining one's daily bread thus becomes a right and a duty of both the individual and the society. This and similar concepts are the key to the Church's social encyclicals.

Of these *Populorum Progressio* is the most crucial. In it Paul VI affirms: 'The fight against poverty is urgent and necessary, but it is not enough. What is needed is the building of a world in which every person without distinction of race, religion or nationality can lead a life which is fully human.' And it is here that the Christian element in the mass media comes in again. I would like to quote, if I may, what I said in 1967 while commenting on this encyclical: 'There is this danger which we must avoid – it is in fact a double pitfall. To glorify the letter without grasping the spirit and to let the initial enthusiasm ebb into oblivion. Against these two real, if not fatal, dangers we must be on our guard.'

Father, give us your nourishment if we prove ourselves deserving of it. Do not give us promotions if we have no qualifications. Do not let us exult without cause. Do not let success seduce us. One loaf of bread per day, not three, not ten. To satisfy our hunger we do not need a sumptuous feast; it is enough to have a reasonable amount of food according to a balanced diet necessary for normal living.

'In order to learn the science of life it is

necessary first to appreciate life.' So declared a Polish thinker of the last century, August Cieszkowski, who worked for almost fifty years on his four volumes of reflections on the prayer which Jesus taught us. In his colossal work (*Ojcze Nasz*, 1848-1889) he developed an extensive series of theological and philosophical considerations on the relationship between God and humanity and especially on the spiritual elements that bind these two protagonists of the cosmos together. Thought and word, feeling and tone, art and science, will and freedom. These means finally lead us to the kingdom of God, the supreme object of all human desires, which is attainable through every means, even through error in so far as it is an intermediary stage on the journey into Truth.

Can even journalists feel reassured by this thought? Yes, provided that the error is not deliberate. The new approach of Cieszkowski bases in the formula 'liberty, equality, fraternity' the right foundation for building a Christian society in which daily bread is not to be a refuge for its members but a normal part of everyday life, even a means of praising God day by day.

Here is also a message of solidarity from Pope John Paul II:

'Let those who are in a position to enjoy a greater share of resources and services be responsible for the weaker members of society and share with them whatever they can. On their part, let the weaker members reciprocate such solidarity by not adopting a passive or negative attitude that might damage the social fabric, but do what they can for the common good' (*Sollicitudo Rei Socialis*).

This line of thinking leads to the economic and ethical aspect and places it in a very broad human perspective. There is also crystallised the meaning of 'being a neighbour' – a theme untiringly insisted upon by the Church in its effort to demonstrate that this should be the first concern of all Christians.

Today's men and women are obsessed with imitating others and then overtaking them in the accumulation of possessions. There is a kind of fever which encourages consumption beyond the limits of reasonable need. One car for one family is no longer enough: one car for each member is becoming the norm. You need a house in town, one by the sea and perhaps one in the country. Shares, bonds, credit cards, savings, deposits, current accounts, all feeding on each other like parasites. Designer clothes, stupid furniture, farcical parties, whimsical travels. We become slaves to these things without even the least resistance.

Deliver us, O Lord, – thus goes a prayer – from the frenzy of wanting and possessing more; give us what is necessary for today, because everything on a table (as the bread, for example) is gift and sweat, and many of our brothers and sisters are beggars of crumbs. Further, open our hearts to the needs of others that we may share our blessings with them.

The media people, more than any other professional category, seem to pose a problem when they set out to do the 'neighbourly act'. Special 'civic virtues' are needed to reconcile work practices with Christianity, practical problems of daily bread with the hope for a better world, and culture with faith. Journalists are not cut off from their surroundings. On the contrary, and especially if they have Christian principles, they can rebuild the bridge between God and our thoroughly secularised society. To transform the world it is enough to heed the central line of advice in the Letter to Diognetus:

'What the soul is in one body, that let the Christians be in the world... The soul lives in the body but does not come from the body; the Christians live in the world but they are not of the world... The soul is locked within the body but it is the soul that sustains the body. The Christians are detained in the prison of the world but it is they who support the world... When put to the test by hunger and thirst, the soul grows stronger.'

Отче наш,

иже еси на небесех,
да светится имя твое,
да придет царстве твое,
да будет воля
твоя яко на небеси и на земли.
Хлеб наш насушни дажд
нам днес,
и остави нам долги наша,
яко же ими оставляет
должником нашим,
и невоведи нас во искушение,
но избави нас от лукаваго.

Амин!

And forgive us
our trespasses

The Russian word *podvig* they say is untranslatable. It means an exceptional gesture. One such gesture was the permission granted by the Soviet authorities for the celebrations to mark 1000 years of faith in the country. The gesture certainly justifies other hopes.

Other extraordinary signs are those symbols of the Christian faith that have survived unscathed under atheistic communism: the churches and the icons. As Pia Compagnini says in her book *The Language of Icons*, the icons of Christ represent 'not just his human nature nor just his divine nature, but the person of the God-man in whom the two natures are unified.' And we begin to grasp what St Paul has taught us: the mystery of Christ 'icon of the invisible God and first-born of all creation' (Colossians 1:15).

The icons narrate sacred history and are an invitation to prayer and love; drawing men and women closer to God. It is a difficult, but not impossible path as demonstrated by the life of the Latvian poetess Elizaveta Jurevna (revolutionary in Czarist Russia, nun in Parisian exile, martyr in the Nazi camp at Ravensbruck), who wrote: 'Only those who discover love may truly claim to be human.' Also the Lord's Prayer tells us the same.

I would venture further and say that the second part of this fundamental we have been meditating upon is a great hymn to the relationship between God and humanity.

After the request for bread, breath and justice, the prayer introduces the themes of being and having. Our debts are not just to be transferred to another account, but to be written off altogether. Forgiven and forgotten. Someone has suggested that, in this respect, the Lord's Prayer becomes a daily baptism as it automatically washes away our sins through direct appeal to God. This interpretation is comforting. It is so to me personally as I have already admitted that I do not know how to pray and as I find a psychological block which makes it difficult for me to go to confession. This part of the prayer must also be comforting to all those who do not know of any intermediaries between their conscience and the mercy of the heavenly Father.

Is there then a legal pact which binds God to us? There is, in a certain sense; and, where debts are concerned, such a deal is practical only in an atmosphere of love. Consider this gospel passage which is unambiguous: 'A certain creditor had two debtors; one owed five hundred denarii, and the other fifty. When they could not pay, he forgave them both. Now which of them will love him more?' Simon answered, 'The one, I suppose, to whom he forgave more.' And he said to him, 'You have judged rightly' (Luke 7:41-43).

I think of this parable every time I hear discussions on international debts, resulting from the loans the neocolonialists gave to poorer nations on the pretext of helping them but in reality for keeping them under their yoke. Well, can we not resolve this problem in the light of the Gospel, with a (political) gesture of love which would create loyalty and trust between the partners? Instead, everyone follows the 'normal' procedure of repeated demands for payment and the inevitably negative replies, with mounting anger and resentment which we journalists report daily without even asking why today's world is incapable of making a (political) gesture of love.

Sometimes we complicate the practice of our faith when it could be made simple with a touch of spontaneity. A century ago Leo Tolstoy tried to devise a way – perhaps somewhat utopian but certainly fundamental – of living the faith: 'They would tell me this. You must believe and pray. But I knew I did not believe much and therefore I was unable to pray... and it was only after rejecting all the learned philosophical and theological treatises and following the saying of Jesus, "If you do not receive me like children, you will not enter the kingdom of heaven", that I suddenly understood what I had never understood before... The strength of Christ's teaching is not in its interpretation of the meaning of life but in its doctrine on life... I believe that my rational life is the light that has been given to me solely that it may shine before men not only in words but also in good works, in order that men may give glory to the Father.'

The Sermon on the Mount summarises Tolstoy's faith which is based on the gospel of Matthew (5:21-48) and emphasises five fundamental rules:

1. Do not get angry but be at peace with all.
2. Do not commit adultery or indulge in thoughts of fornication.
3. Do not swear by anything or anyone.
4. Do not resist the wicked and neither judge nor condemn.
5. Do not discriminate against foreigners but love them as your own countrymen.

The doors of heaven will open to anyone who strictly adheres to these precepts, Tolstoy concludes, borrowing the words of Jesus: 'Be you as perfect as your Father in heaven.'

Rationally speaking – outside any religious frame of reference – such an interpretation of the world expresses an absolute sense of justice. Those who forgive the trespasses of both friends and enemies offer the greatest expression of love.

Chinese

在天我等父者我等願爾名見
聖爾國臨格爾旨承行於地如
於天焉我等望爾與我我
日用糧而免我債如我亦免負
我債者又不我許陷於誘感乃
救我於凶惡亞孟

As we forgive those who trespass against us

Forgiveness is almost an unknown experience in society nowadays. Jesus has given us any number of examples and motives for forgiveness, but modern men and women are proving indifferent. However, we are not slack in making promises: 'Lord, if you forgive us our trespasses we will do the same to our neighbour.' We make promises after having been assured of God's benevolence to us. In his boundless mercy, we are sure God will hear us.

What holds us back from acts of forgiveness? Pride which is the mother of all hypocrisies, someone has suggested. And hypocrisy is also found wherever there is a lack of charity and goodwill. It was for this reason that Jesus branded as hypocrites the scribes and Pharisees who were meticulous about the tax on insignificant products and then flouted the more serious aspects of the law such as justice, mercy and faith (Matthew 23:23). And equally hypocritical are those who proclaim their Christian faith and then form themselves into secret cliques and societies that do not encourage an open and responsible life style. With many people the shaking of hands during Mass is purely formal – not at all offering each other the sign of peace!

Is it perhaps the loss of simplicity in our dealings with each other that has brought about the weakening of the religious sense in our society? In this respect we would do well to heed the example of older civilizations. In China, for example, they still follow a combination of religion (Buddhism), philosophy (Taoism) and behaviour (Confucianism), drawing from each discipline what is best for personal formation. And to them it is so natural that there is a Chinese saying that 'the three religions are but one'.

It is another way of stating that to observe the important ethical principles is to adhere closely to the *Tao*, the path of the just. The absence of the priestly class and the prevalence of a strong sense of religious individualism, characteristic of the Chinese mentality today, have produced positive factors like the popularity of personal prayer (spontaneous, not stereotype, especially for one's ancestors) and the tendency to collective action (accepted not suffered, for the good of the village or town). In this way the remission of debts, the forgiveness of wrongs, assumes a clearly defined meaning for all men and women of goodwill.

Let us now take a look at what really happens in the gathering and reporting of news. Murder, rape, theft, accidents, conferences, meetings, inaugurations, scandals. Anything. It's all grist to the mill. So far so good. But the problem begins with the actual style of reporting which tends to be riddled with clichés and meaningless expressions. And what is worse is the change of roles. The reporter becomes the judge; the criminal or the accused becomes a star. The authorities of law and order are subjected to pressures and accusations beyond the limits of reason. Another aberration is to make a spectacle out of a news story. The reporter ceases to be an observer and becomes a participant, then an unwitting spokesperson and defender of crime itself.

Let it be stressed that every individual – including confessed criminals – has a right to protect his or her personal dignity, for every human being possesses a conscience. There also exists a collective dignity which should be safeguarded for the sake of professional integrity. Christianity teaches us to offer the other cheek besides and beyond forgiving those who offend us. But we must be equally anxious to ensure that the suffering of the victims and the distress of their relatives are not aggravated by insensitive reporting. Here we must be guided by our professional ethics. The problem is how to apply it in our work from day to day.

I recall an old friend who, at the beginning of my journalistic career, gave me the formula for turning out a good piece: inform and form. But, after all these years I realize that, while it is easy enough to inform, it is difficult and more complex to form public opinion. One is up against a system which has numerous checks and stops to thwart any personal initiative. This is true of any editorial office. They call it 'editorial policy' (read 'conformism'). And so the system flourishes. Here the conformists win always.

In the Hebrew culture the word *hob* stood as much for a debt as for a sin. In older times, and up until recent years, a transgression of the law (sin) brought with it a profound sense of shame both for the transgressor and for his or her family members. Today the mentality is different. The sense of sin is no longer there in our permissive society which absolves – even exalts – those who cause scandals. Values have been turned upside down: simplicity is seen as weakness, truth is turned into arrogance, morality is abandoned in the pursuit of pleasures.

Are we then witnessing the death of the spirit? No, the spirit lives as long as there is at least one just person.

Japanese

天においでになるわた
したちの父よ、み名が聖と
されますように。みくにが
来ますように。みむねが天
におこなわれるように地に
もおこなわれますように。
わたしたちの日々のかてを
きょうもお与えください。
わたしたちが負いめをもつ
人をゆるすように、わたし
たちの負いめをおゆるしく
ださい。わたしたちをここ
ろみにあわせず、悪からお
救いください。
　　　　アメン。

And lead us not
into temptation

Deliver us, O Lord, from the spell of treacherous thoughts. We might pray thus in order to be rid of one of the worst forms of torment known to man. We all have our own. It is related that Hirohito, the 124th emperor of Japan (1901-1989), did not believe in the tradition of his divine origins going back to Amaterasu, the daughter of the Sun. This was a scandal to the court at Tokyo. But it rendered him civilised and enlightened in the eyes of the West. His intellectual friends found in his regal personality the perfect blend of the ideographs *Hiro* (great, generous, kind) and *Hito* (perfection, benevolence, humanity). History does not seem to confirm the same perfection of virtue in his use of power which was scarcely celestial. No matter. The deed does not always correspond to the ideal.

We often talk about shaping the world according to our liking while we ignore it as it really is. Why do we lull ourselves in the cradle of illusion? It is like being on the stage of the Japanese classical theatre with its perfect fusion of recitative, music and singing, dazzling in pomp and circumstance, but devoid of any social content. We would be better off with *Kabuki*, a more recent form of Japanese theatre, where we can feel the popular pulse which, albeit licentious on occasion, is always fresh and lively. All forms of entertainment ought to provide an escape, so argue some people. But it is a mistaken idea. Any form of entertainment, with its powers of persuasion, is an opportunity for inculcating sound principles and spreading good ideas.

It is important to take due account of the creative tension of the artists and the propulsive power of any show. It is no less important to keep a watchful eye and offer criticism and suggestions in order to encourage and enliven a performance. Music for example, has become an extraordinarily powerful force in our times. Contrast the positive effects produced by classical music, the opera, jazz, folk, country and western, with the negative influences of pop and rock.

And how should we react to a film or book that distorts the truth about a person or event? In our judgement we should use reason instead of zeal and fanaticism, especially the religious variety, as they only succeed in doing irreparable damage. Leaving aside the content of *Satanic Verses*, it is instructive to recall the anger of Islam which has issued a death sentence against the author Salman Rushdie. There are times when it is better to react with silence and indifference. This would prevent the kind of publicity that would be eagerly exploited by scandalmongers as happened in the case of the film *The Last Temptation*. A realistic portrayal of Christ is not the same as a subjective interpretation which has no time for tradition and truth.

Who then was Jesus, man and God, who allowed himself to be tempted? And how can we fight against a society which we ourselves have fed with permissiveness and decadence? In this society anything goes: genetic manipulation, squandering of natural resources, destruction of the environment. All this is done in the name of freedom to experiment which in point of fact degrades the human race. It is certainly not God who tempts us. It is instead we who are incapable of keeping watch over our safety. 'Watch and pray that you may not enter into temptation. The spirit indeed is willing, but the flesh is weak' (Matthew 26:41).

We are also obsessed with possessing everything. 'But those who desire to be rich fall into temptation, into a snare, into many senseless and hurtful desires that plunge men into ruin and destruction' (1 Timothy 6:9). It might be useful in this context to recall the distinction made by the Capuchin mystic and stigmatist Padre Pio. 'There are two contrasting types,' he used to say. 'Temptations which are well and truly a corruption of the spirit, and they come from the devil; and temptations which are trials sent by God to test the believer.'

For those who work in social communications temptation lies in wait in a thousand and one deceptive forms and shapes. One typical example is the temptation to attack religion in the hope of stirring up controversy and attracting publicity. And in such circumstances the differing cultural backgrounds and degrees of tolerance among religious denominations are major factors. Religious tolerance and intolerance are two sides of the same coin. Another analogy would be that of the litmus paper. Both tolerance and intolerance test one's capacity to love God genuinely and to resist all temptation.

Temptation as such – theologians clarify – does not constitute sin. It becomes culpable once we give our mental consent, and that is the downfall of the flesh. Let no one presume to be safe.

Irish

´Ar nAthair

atá ar neamh,
go naofar d'ainm,
go dtaga do ríocht,
gp ndéantar do thoil ar an
    talamh,
mar a dheantar ar neamh.
´Ar n-arán laethúil tabhair
    dúinn inniu,
agus maith dúinn ár bhfiacha,
mar a mhaithimidne dár
    bhféichiúna féin,
agus ná lig sinn i gcathú,
ach saor sinn ó olc.

Welsh

Ein Tad

y sy yn y nefoedd,
santeiddier dy enw,
deled dy deyrnas,
bydded dy ewyllys ar y ddaear
    megis yn y nef.
Dyro inni heddiw eein bara
    beunyddiol,
a maddau inni ein dyledion,
fel y maddeuwn ninnau i'n
    dyledwyr.
Ac nac arwain ni i brofedigaeth,
eithr gwared ni rhag drwg.

Scottish

´Ar nAthair

a tá air nèamh,
Gu naomhaichear d'ainm.
Thigeadh do rìoghachd.
Deanar do thoil air an talamh,
    mar a nithear air neamh
Tabhair dhuinn ar fiachan,
    amhuil a mhaitheas sinne d'ar
    luchdfiach
Agus na leig ann am buaireadh
    sinn;
Ach saor sinn o olc:
Oir is leatsa an rìoghachd
Agus a' cumhachd
Agus a' ghloìr
Gu sìrruidh.
Amen

But deliver us
from evil

On 23 January 1989, the feast of St Francis de Sales, patron of journalists, the following words were addressed to us by the Cardinal Archbishop of Milan, Carlo Maria Martini:

'To be free and impartial is difficult indeed. Not to realise this is already a mistake. If it is difficult to be impartial, let us at least guard against interpretations that are deliberately biased. When we are in the wrong let us not justify our stand purely to save face. But let us instead have a sense of humour and face the unvarnished truth.'

But 450 years before the Milanese archbishop, St Thomas More had composed this prayer:

'Grant me, O Lord, good health and the good temper to keep it. Let me never be vexed, let me never complain, let me never take myself too seriously. Give me a sense of humour and the grace to make the best of a bad job. Grant me the gift of joy and help me to make others share it.'

Let us meditate, fellow journalists and all others, and live by these wise counsels.

Obviously, for a Christian journalist, the most serious breach would be the distortion and suppression of truth as the leader and the feature constitute an effective moral weapon. Those with business interests or investments may be tempted to compromise their conscience or to be economical with truth. It is therefore necessary to examine one's conscience daily. Consistent and honest reporting appears to be the basic problem which plagues the relations between the papers and the public as also between the Church and the media.

Humanity probably acts against life's natural laws under the influence of evil. In forms that are unmistakable, evil permeates our life at every level, affecting us in subtle and unsuspecting ways. It is bad to accept bribes; it is bad to evade tax; it is bad to exploit a sexual scandal to the embarrassment of everyone concerned; and naturally, it is bad to steal, to give false testimony, to kill. Evil lurks in secret places, but no one can claim to have been forced to do evil.

In the short letter handed down to us from a silent and inflexible apostle – I allude to James the Less – there are some scorching words against hypocrites: 'Each person is tempted when he is lured and enticed by his own desire. Then desire when it has conceived gives birth to sin; and sin when it is full-grown brings forth death' (James 1:14-15). A little further on, the letter warns us about the use of our tongue – this two-edged sword – from which issues wisdom, or falsehood which generates conflict, ambition, envy, discord, jealousy, slander, violence.

Often the media willingly give time and space to wild tongues and slanderous voices which encourage polemics of every kind. Incredible as it may seem, this phenomenon is nowhere more verifiable than in sports where one would expect to find tolerance and respect for each other. Sports has become so commercialized that excellence and sportsmanship are no longer esteemed as before. Behind the walls and the towers there is a great emptiness now.

Let us return to the main theme of deliverance from evil. In this last verse, according to Cyprian of Carthage, 'we include all the adversities with which the enemy threatens us in this world. We shall certainly be saved from them if God comes to our aid when we invoke him and ask his help.' The decision therefore is really up to us. God is our destiny and our role is to give expression to it through our lives. Consider these words written on the wall of a convent:

'Life is for seeking God,
death is for finding him,
eternity is for possessing him.'

It is a formula which is as admirable as it is simple. It then follows that human life is enriched through drawing closer to the supernatural. Death is but the starting point of eternal life, and our life on this earth is merely a preparation for that death. Such logic makes sense only to those who believe.

At this juncture we must briefly consider the moral question, both from the Christian and the general point of view. Our conscience and reason are forged by the continuous interaction of society which finally is responsible for the formation of its members. How then are we to tackle the present moral bankruptcy of our society? We must learn from children who quite naturally know how to tell right from wrong, good from evil, the just from the unjust. It is a matter of clarity of conscience and language, irrespective of secular or religious contexts. In a world where everything from kidneys to conscience can be bought, it is cause for celebration to come across people who refuse to put their conscience up for sale.

Secular thinking nowadays seems to accept any new fad as an unavoidable stage in human progress. It is hardly true. Moral reasoning and religious principles cannot be separated. The great experiences of humanity have always been testimonies of God's presence and power. Without conversion there can be no moral growth. Without reason there can be no growth in knowledge. And without faith there can be no inner freedom.

In his book *Teach Us to Pray* Enrico

Masseroni has this to say about the last verse of the Our Father: 'There is no freedom without deliverance, no victory without struggle, no life without death. Deliver us from the evil that is known to us and from the evil that hides under other names. Deliver us above all from our inclination to live a life devoid of any idealism. Deliver us from presumption. Fill us with your spirit so that, freed at last from our self-importance and presumed virtues, we may be able to enjoy your fatherly love.'

Faith in Christ frees us from the slavery of evil and offers us the freedom to choose. This implies readiness for action since 'a man is justified by works and not by faith alone' (James 2:24). Thus it is that the Christian becomes chief guarantor of freedom in its full sense of individual and collective moral responsibility. For those who work in the media freedom is a treasure to be cherished and to be used prudently and responsibly.

Freedom enables us to define our personalities and our sense of solidarity with our fellow human beings of every creed, race and nationality. In the case of secular journalists freedom implies a particularly serious undertaking because it demands courage. And in the case of Christian journalists the responsibility is even greater. For they become either stumbling blocks or witnesses to the faith. They are stumbling blocks if they occupy key editorial posts and reduce everything to routine. And they are witnesses for their times if they are able to analyse society and help it to improve in every aspect.

Arabic

أَبَانَا ٱلَّذِي فِي
ٱلسَّمَوَاتِ . لِيَتَقَدَّسِ
ٱسْمُكَ . لِيَأْتِ مَلَكُوتُكَ .
لِتَكُنْ مَشِيئَتُكَ كَمَا فِي
ٱلسَّمَاءِ وَعَلَى ٱلْأَرْضِ .
خُبْزَنَا كَفَافَنَا أَعْطِنَا ٱلْيَوْمَ
ٱلْيَوْمَ . وَٱغْفِرْ لَنَا خَطَايَانَا
كَمَا نَغْفِرُ نَحْنُ لِمَنْ أَخْطَأَ
إِلَيْنَا . وَلَا تُدْخِلْنَا
ٱلتَّجَارِبَ . لَكِنْ نَجِّنَا مِنَ

ٱلشِّرِّيرِ . آمِينَ .

Hebrew

אבינו שבשמים
יתקדש שמך
תבא מלכותך
יעשה רצונך
כמו בשמים
כן בארץ
את לחם חקנו
תן לנו היום
וסלח לנו
את חבותינו
כאשר סלחנו
גם אנחנו לחיבינו
ואל תביאנו לידי נסיון
כי אם חלצנו מן הרע
כי לך הממלכה
והגבורה והתפארת
לעולמי עולמים
אמן

Amen

What then is the Lord's Prayer? It is a prayer of peace. It is a burst of joy, a declara-tion of trust, a yearning for peace, an expression of solidarity, a universal prayer. Well, at the end of this rapid commentary on the words Jesus dictated to us through Matthew and Luke, it seems to me fitting and necessary to place side by side two ribs of Adam, the Arabs and the Jews, in the hope that the old wounds between them may soon be healed by the spirit of peace. This is the cry of the *anawim*, the poor of the world, for the vocation of Christians is to be messengers of peace. There is no other means of salvation. Only hope and faith allying themselves in love can save us and future generations.

We are about to bid farewell. And every prayer ends with an acclamation, a wish, or a supplication. The word *Amen* is usually translated as 'so be it', but it can also mean 'I stand firm' or 'this is the truth'. This form is in use in synagogues, churches and mosques as it sums up the authentic spirit of the monotheistic religions.

But, the Lord's Prayer has a universal application. Its horizons are vast enough to encompass all nations and religions. It is the best prayer for the hour of agony which lasts till the end of the world. Life, growth, death. But what hope is there for such thoughts in our irrational, materialistic, restless society?

You need at least a word or a gesture of love in order to attain the contemplation of God. As in a human relationship of love two beings think and act in perfect harmony, so in a religious context we must cultivate the virtues of selflessness, understanding, kindness, charity. But in either case the essential basis of love is sincerity. For in loving, as in dying, we cannot pretend. Let us therefore in total sincerity speak to our heavenly Father in the words of the most beautiful and memorable prayer that Jesus has taught us.

St Francis of Assisi used to recommend this prayer to his brothers and to the townspeople – he asked them to say it twenty-four times in the morning and as many times as possible throughout the day. Likewise, St Clare exhorted her sisters to recite this prayer because it was as simple and clear as it was profound and universal. In the Christian tradition the Our Father is certainly the most cherished prayer.

So it has been, so be it, so it will be. Through the will of God the world will finally achieve the peace that is longed for. This the Fathers of the Church assure us. But will everyone enjoy it, in equal measure? 'And the harvest of righteousness is sown in peace by those who make peace' (James 3:18). We are called to work for peace.

Finding solutions to conflicts is obviously the speciality of politicians. Nonetheless, we journalists cannot relinquish the direct responsibility of informing and forming world opinion on the state of affairs in trouble spots around the world. A case in point is the tension between the Palestinians and Israelis. The media seem to have done nothing but aggravate the problem by stressing only the causes of disagreement rather than offering a serious analysis of all the factors. Reporters often give the impression of siding with either one or the other group of the inhabitants of this disturbed land which witnessed the birth, preaching and death of Jesus of Nazareth and which still nurtures diverse languages that have sprung from the same root. Peace is *shalom* in Hebrew and *salam* in Arabic. Tragically, no one seems prepared to find a univocal sound for this word and above all to transform it into actual peace and prosperity for both peoples. Where there is no peace may hope germinate in prayer.

The poet Kahlil Gibran, a son of the Lebanon, another tormented country, was inspired by the great monotheistic religions and wrote his own version of the Our Father. In it he gives the finest expression to our longing for the world of heaven:

'Holy is your name. May your will be done in us and in the universe. Give us your bread for today. In your kindness forgive us and bestow on us the grace to forgive one another. Guide us to you and in the darkness extend to us your hand from heaven. For yours is the kingdom and in you is the source of our strength and our fulfilment.'

What I find particularly pleasing is the request for reciprocal forgiveness which involves everyone. The art of mutual forgiveness is something we must all practise without prejudices, pretensions, or reservations.

And this is where I stop. The rest I leave to others. It is getting late. We finalise the pages. We put the finishing touches to the radio and television programmes. And now, feeling as if I had been making notes for a spiritual testament, I realize that writing is a marvellous career, despite the anxieties and inconveniences entailed in doing justice to the profession. I feel the weight of years. I am aware of my inadequacy in dealing with world events. There is within me the niggling anxiety about an unfinished quest. There is also the secret regret for botched jobs, for what I could have done, and for what I failed to do. But I do not intend to give up.

I reread a letter from a friend who tells me to look at the affairs of our journalistic life with renewed hope. He writes: 'In my small way I share the burden of journalism, but I thank God for it, and I really don't have any complaints. From a Christian point of view, I am very happy to work among books, magazines, and discs, I can *love others through the service of truth,* as stressed so often by James Alberione, the founder of the Society of St Paul and other Pauline congregations.'

Have I succeeded in weaving a thread of possibility, if not of optimism or fervour in these notes on the Lord's Prayer? I do not know. It is for others to say. But of one thing I am certain: Christian hope never dies; it is intimately linked to our faith in the human being, as evidenced in the creative spirit and undeniable achievements of this complex creature that dominates the earth.

Well, I would like to sign off and then take a long rest, but I am restless. Within me there is an agitation for producing more. I know that otherwise it would be an unjustified surrender, an act of cowardice, an illogical step for one who professes to be a Christian and who has received numerous gifts from the Lord. The gift of a wife, the gift of three children, the gift of a profession.

Time passes. Night is about to fall and the light is fading. And the words linger in the heart like the memory of loved ones.

Postscript

The prayer to God the Father is never more satisfying than when it corresponds to a joyful occasion in our life. A priest friend maintains that a Christian should never be sad because it would be a contradiction of God's sanctifying grace. God loves us, untiringly. Such love should not be repaid through acts devoid of charity. I use the word charity deliberately because of its precise meaning – an attitude of understanding and fellowship towards others as also an impulse of generosity and kindness towards those in need. Charity is a complement to the very beautiful concept denoted by the word love.

Modern society often confuses love with eros, which is hedonism based on utilitarianism and therefore essentially on materialism – our philosophies that recognize no truths except their self idolatry. But our society stands in need of education, intelligence, justice, values, idealism – and this is where the Christian man and woman can make their contribution inspired by love. *Be a neighbour* at every level, therefore, with a challenge of the heart both in the family and in the community.

In the family this challenge requires a conversion (turning towards God) and a change in our personal life style in order to render more effective the pact of love sealed by the sacrament of marriage.

In the community being a neighbour means the curbing of excessive individualism and narrow-mindedness so that there can be closer co-operation with the various institutions and associations in the spirit of what the Gospel teaches: 'A new commandment I give to you, that you love one another; even as I have loved you, that you also love one another. By this all men will know that you are my disciples, if you have love for one another' (John 13:34-35).

Hence the boundlessness of Christian love which embraces every human being as brother or sister, free and equal, never, but never to be treated differently because of race or wealth: under the cross there are no reserved seats for the privileged, and in the halls of politics and the boardrooms of the media there are no supermen.

In this spirit of charity, and in accordance with the last verse of Dante's *Paradiso* where 'love which moves the sun and the stars' urges us to live in 'virtue and wisdom', let us dare to pray yet again: *Our Father...*

Swahili

Baba Yetu

uliye mbinguni,
jina lako litukuzwe.
Ufalme wako ufike.
Utakalo lifanyike duniani
kama mbinguni.
Utupe leo mkate wetu wa kila
    siku.
Utusamehe makosa yetu,
kama tunavyowasamehe na sisi
    waliotukosea.
Usitutie katika kishawishi,
lakini utuopoe maovuni.
Amina

A JOURNALIST
LOOKS AT THE PARABLES

In these pages Italian journalist Angelo Montonati offers his personal interpretation of the parables of Jesus. They give him the cue to discuss some issues that particularly affect our society. The stories Jesus told are shown to be made-to-measure stories also for our times. With their touch of humour and irony, they penetrate the tangled mess of our contradictions and illuminate the confused hopes and fears of our century.

Thus the story of the workers in the vineyard becomes the parable of the trade unionists. The lesson of the talents is transformed into a satirical account of the error of burying ourselves in idleness. Lazarus and the rich man represent the Third World and the West being judged by God. In a society where collective blame dilutes any sense of personal sin, responsibility is the lesson to be learned from the parable of the good seed and weeds. And in the famous parable of the prodigal son the emphasis shifts from the tragedy of the son's sin to the logic of the father's prodigal love. What a moving image of God who, aching with love for humanity, 'runs wild with joy' every time one of us decides to turn over a new leaf.

ISBN 085439 385 4   144 pp.   £4.95